LANCASHIRE
NORTH OF THE SANDS
IN OLD PHOTOGRAPHS

LANCASHIRE
NORTH OF THE SANDS
IN OLD PHOTOGRAPHS

COLLECTED BY

JOHN GARBUTT
AND JOHN MARSH

ALAN SUTTON

Alan Sutton Publishing Limited
Phoenix Mill · Far Thrupp · Stroud · Gloucestershire

First published 1991

British Library Cataloguing in Publication Data

Lancashire North of the sands in old photographs.
I. Garbutt, John, *1932–*
II. Marsh, John, *1931–*
942.78

ISBN 0-75090-026-1

05362094

This book is dedicated to
Barbara and Jean
Helpers in so many ways

Front Cover Illustration: ULVERSTON PARADE, 1905.

Typeset in 9/10 Korinna.
Typesetting and origination by
Alan Sutton Publishing Limited.
Printed in Great Britain by
The Bath Press, Avon.

CONTENTS

BAPTISM AT CARTMEL PRIORY, 1902, by Sawyer of Kendal.

INTRODUCTION

Lancashire North of the Sands ceased to exist in name on All Fools Day, 1 April 1974, when the County of Cumbria included the area within its boundaries. As all the photographs in this book pre-date 1974 by some decades it seemed appropriate to the authors to use the title which graced the Furness and Cartmel areas for centuries.

The boundaries of these ancient lands were laid down in antiquity and can still be traced today, in spite of bureaucratic attempts to tidy them away. They are the River Duddon in the north-west, as far as the watershed, and the River Rothay to Windermere, Windermere lake to Newby Bridge, Windermere lake to Ghyll Head and the River Winster to the sea at Meathop. They are sensible geographic boundaries that anyone can understand. None of the lake of Windermere was in the county of Lancashire and all of the lake of Coniston was. The boundaries were once the borders of baronies and marked the extent of the intrusion of the rich county of Lancashire into the poorer counties of Cumberland and Westmorland. The 'Three Shires Stone' on the watershed at Wrynose Pass said everything in naming only Lancashire.

The early story of both Cartmel and Furness has yet to be written. There are a few tantalizing clues to the story in pre-Roman, Roman and 'Dark Ages' times but nothing to project the history in any meaningful manner. So much is supposition. The formation of both areas appears to pre-date the Normans. In medieval times both were homes to substantial monastic interests – the Cistercian Abbey of St Mary of Furness and the Augustinian Priory of Cartmel. After the Reformation, and until the present day, the land was divided into private estates, the largest holding of which was the land of the Prestons of Furness Abbey and Holker, now consolidated in the Cavendish family at Holker.

The seventeenth century saw the formation of the Quaker movement by George Fox who, in 1652, came from Leicestershire to Swarthmoor and the Fell family. It is said that Swarthmoor Hall, near Ulverston, became the 'headquarters' for the spread of the Quaker movement. Quakerism had a greater impact on neighbouring Kendal than on Ulverston itself.

The eighteenth century witnessed the expansion of trade by sea at the two ports of Ulverston and Greenodd. Ulverston acquired a canal which was proclaimed to be the 'shortest, straightest and deepest in England' by some and the 'shortest, broadest and deepest in England' by others. (When Greenodd's days as a port were coming to an end there were plans to extend Ulverston canal to that village.)

During the nineteenth century the exploitation of the iron ore deposits in Furness produced a revolution in transport, work patterns and population. Some of the first experimentations in the use of iron for industrial purposes were carried out by John Wilkinson at Lindale in Cartmel. The new borough of Barrow-in-Furness, which was developed during the nineteenth century, produced a new race of 'industrial' barons. The Furness Railway changed the coast line and much else for ever. The iron and steel works at Askam, Ulverston and Barrow and the huge shipyards at Barrow provided work for many people and there was a big influx of workers from other areas which made a marked difference to the Furness population. (Barrow-in-Furness is not to be found in this book as it was a separate borough and of sufficient size to deserve a separate publication.)

The reader will find the sea and sea transport mentioned at the beginning and end of the book. The sea, and the sands, form a large part of Cartmel and Furness history. Many lost their lives approaching or leaving the area when the main routes were by sea or by sands. The Victorians and Edwardians could enjoy a short sea journey to and from Lancashire South of the Sands (i.e. Blackpool, Fleetwood and Morecambe) on their trips from and to Lancashire North of the Sands. This is a facility lost to us today. The Furness Railway, tied into the rise and decline of the Furness iron and steel trade, became part of the LMS Railway in 1923. The holiday trade, so much part of the Furness Railway scheme of development, never produced the income which industry had. Ships on the sea and ships on the lakes, with interconnecting trains and coaches and specially built hotels, produced package holidays of a special kind in southern Lakeland that not everyone appreciated. Most of the Furness Railway holiday developments took place within Furness itself, the steamers sailing into neighbouring Lancashire South of the Sands and Westmorland (at Bowness and Ambleside) almost as if they were foreign parts.

This is the land of the boyhood of the authors who in many ways were fortunate to experience the late 1930s and the 1940s when 'adventure' was easily obtained, the war was a long way away (it came a bit closer when Barrow and Grange were bombed) and society was so very different from today. It was then possible to cycle and walk about the district with a freedom that motor transport now denies. The fells were virtually empty, the villages occupied by locals whose families had lived there for generations, the churches were full for services and left open when not being used, and a spirit of community was to be found that has since been all but lost through circumstances which most of the locals had little control over.

The photographers whose work makes up this book are named wherever possible with the photographs they have taken. Commercial photographers at Grange-over-Sands, Ulverston, Dalton and Barrow produced a wealth of material, the quality of which was very high indeed. Edward Sankey of Barrow towers above all others in the breadth and quality of his work. (It is understood that his photographic archive is still intact and must surely be worthy of preservation by the County archive or museum service.) Some of the photographs are private family pictures. So much social history material of the latter kind is lost when houses are cleared after death, etc., but fortunately some has survived. We are pleased to use pictures from these surviving personal collections as they offer a unique personal angle on the history of the district.

So many of the Victorian and Edwardian famous from the Cartmel and Furness area are now unknown to most of the population. For instance, the Coward family of Foxfield, related to one of the authors, were tenants of Viscount William Henry Cross PC, GCB, GCSI, LLD, FRS, JP, Secretary of State for India from 1886 to 1892, who lived nearby at Eccle Riggs. His house is now more famous for its bar snacks and swimming pool and Viscount Cross is known only to historians. Street names in Ulverston, Dalton and Barrow, towns that were being greatly expanded during the lifetime of the person named, now record such as Brogden, Schneider, Cavendish and Ramsden. The large monument on Hoad Hill, Ulverston (would the planners permit such a thing today?) reminds us of John Barrow. The Quakers would not have wished for, but have, a seventeenth-century shrine to George Fox and the Fell family at Swarthmoor. William Wordworth's poetry was inspired by the River Duddon and he and his brother were educated at Hawkshead. John Ruskin lived much of his life at Brantwood on Coniston Lake and was very much involved in the local community. The National Trust came out of High Furness with Ruskin and his friend Rawnsley. Beatrix Potter lived in the area and found many of her animal characters and scenes hereabouts. Arthur Ransome lived in and wrote about the Cartmel Fell and High Furness areas in his books. Stan Laurel (of Laurel and Hardy fame) was born and lived part of his boyhood in Ulverston. Donald Campbell was tragically killed breaking a waterspeed record on Coniston. This book touches on several of these but also includes many who were in no way famous but were as much part of the Furness and Cartmel scene of their day.

Part of the proceeds of the book will be given to the funds of the Lake District Art Gallery and Museum Trust, Abbot Hall, Kendal. The Trust has provided a museum service for southern Cumbria since the Second World War, working with the local authorities, and saving one of Kendal's most attractive buildings in the process.

John Garbutt and John Marsh – Summer 1991

Grange and Cartmel

955

MUSSELS, COCKLES, SHRIMPS AND FLUKES were at one time taken from the bay at Grange-over-Sands by a number of families of fisherfolk. In the picture can be seen the jumbo (the board with two handles) and the cram (the three-pronged fork for lifting the cockles as the jumbo brought them to the surface). The method was too efficient, with 'overfishing' threatening the whole industry at one time.

THE MORECAMBE STEAMER leaves the Bayley Lane pier. The steamer service lasted until 1910 – it is reported that the last steamer to call was the *Sunbeam*. There was a strong body of opinion in Grange that boat and train loads of, mostly Yorkshire, holiday-makers should not be brought to the town. The boat owners, the railway company and a number of Grange traders thought otherwise.

LARGE PRAWNER YACHTS from Morecambe, shown in this photograph by G. Wilson of Grange, also brought many people to Grange as part of a 'round the bay' trip. It is likely that many of the boats were built by Crosfields at Arnside.

THE BAYLEY LANE JETTY, C. 1870, existed before the pier was built by the Morecambe Steamboat Company. There is no promenade and the railway lines are open to the sea.

THE BAYLEY LANE PIER at Myrtle Bank in the late nineteenth century. This was the original pier built for the Morecambe Bay steamers. In 1893 a larger pier was built at Clare House. For a short time both piers existed together.

SUMMER HOLIDAY-MAKERS, children with their nanny and the Clare House pier in the early 1920s by Matthews of Bradford.

HOLIDAY-MAKERS FROM MORECAMBE, disembarking at Clare House pier and passing families being touted to join a sea trip, can be seen in this Frith photograph republished by J.L. Butler of Grange.

THE STORM of 8 October 1896, with the sea showings its power. It is reported that Richard Bush purchased a pier from Piel (see p. 158) and re-erected it to make the Clare House pier in 1893. From an early date the pier suffered from storms such as this.

MANY YEARS OF STORM DAMAGE and, in later years, neglect as the holiday trade changed resulted in the Clare House pier becoming little more than a jetty as can be seen in this Salmon of Sevenoaks picture of about 1930.

A SHARP STEWART 0–6–0, rebuilt by the Furness Railway and seen here taking a train from Grange towards Ulverston, approaches the Bayley Lane crossing about 1910. A first class return ticket from Grange to Ulverston was 2s. 11d. A Thursday 'market day return' was 1s. 3d.

CHILDREN AT PLAY on the rocky beach at Grange. The Clare House pier is in the background of this photograph by A.W. Hankinson of Main Street, Grange, c. 1910.

THE PROMENADE with the tea-rooms and the bandstand, c. 1905, by Pettitt of Keswick. The Promenade was very new, having been extended from Bayley Lane in the years 1902 to 1904. The Furness Railway Company had earlier built a small promenade from the station and this was extended with the help of generous financial support from Harold Porritt. The bandstand was moved to the park gardens in 1928.

BERNERS CLOSE WAS ORIGINALLY KNOWN AS 'BURNERS CLOSE'. The original house was converted into a hotel by J.H. Midgley JP in about 1883 when he acquired it from A. Mason the auctioneer. The hotel was extensively rebuilt in subsequent years to produce the building in the second photograph, taken in about 1930 by A. and L. Slingsby of Grange.

A VICTORIAN EVENT at St Paul's parish church, Grange-over-Sands. The church was built in 1853 to the design of T. Barry of Liverpool for £2,100, and this photograph was taken during its early years. The first clock has yet to appear in the church wall. It was reported that the first parson to the new church, the Revd Wilson Rigg, approached his new parish across the sands by coach from Lancaster and in doing so lost all his possessions when his coach overturned.

THE PICTURE POSTCARD opposite by Wildt and Kray of London depicts the holiday-maker to Grange-over-Sands. The card was dated July 1912. Many Grange residents hated this image of their town.

Arrived safely at
Grange-over-Sands

GRANGE STATION was built in 1872 to replace what had been described as 'little more than tin sheds'. The first picture shows a train from the south with what appears to be a Sharp Stewart 0–6–0 engine entering the station; the second, by Masons of Grange, a rebuilt version of the Sharp Stewart 0–6–0 with a goods train on the 'Up' line from Ulverston in about 1910.

OUR LOCAL EXPRESS
Grange to Kendal
and back in one day

KENDAL TOMMY, the Grange to Kendal train, is the butt of the joke in this postcard by 'Cynicus' of Tayport, Fife, who printed many good-humoured digs at Edwardian life. The Kendal train was housed in the engine shed and siding at Grange and ran, via the Hincaster branch line from Arnside, until May 1942.

THE LARGE DUCK POND in the ornamental gardens. The gardens were built on the site of what had been a creek from the sea, possibly an ancient port. The pond soon became a major attraction with a collection of seabirds and waterfowl. H.T. Mason of Grange pictured mother and children feeding the swans about 1910.

THE GRANGE CARNIVAL is pictured here in 1923 with an earlier type of entry in the form of a decorated cycle which contrasts with the then modern decorated motor lorry. Note the solid tyres, and the tableau on the back.

WILLIAM AND JOHN MOSSOP, 'Grocers, confectioners and fancy bread bakers', who also had a mill at Lindale, had their fine business premises in the centre of the village. The building remains today with everything nearby changed almost beyond recognition. The firm also offered a door-to-door service from their 'bread cart' which is pictured below on the Kents Bank Road with Mr W. Mossop.

MAIN STREET, GRANGE at the turn of the century, as photographed by James Atkinson of Ulverston. Note Hankinson the photographer's large sign. George Samuel Hankinson was the first to be buried in the new cemetery (of 1881). On the right hand side, next to

Warhurst's ironmongery shop, was the Grange post office (see p. 26). In the background a charabanc coach stands with boarding ladder down.

THE CROWN HOTEL, Grange-over-Sands, photographed on a carte-de-visite in the 1880s. For many years the inn was owned by the Westwood family until it was purchased by Yates and Co. It was so badly damaged by fire in 1908 it had to be demolished and rebuilt.

THE POSTMEN AND STAFF at Grange-over-Sands post office in 1905 when there were eight collections between 5.55 a.m. and 9 p.m., three deliveries between 6.30 a.m. and 5 p.m., and even a delivery at 6.30 a.m. and collection at 5.15 p.m. on Sundays. The post office was open for business six days a week from 7 a.m. to 8 p.m. and on Sundays from 8 a.m. to 10 a.m.

THE CLOCK TOWER, built 1912, with a member of the Lancashire Constabulary on duty watching the motor traffic outside the rebuilt Crown Hotel. This Atkinson and Pollitt of Kendal picture dates from about 1930.

THE BOTTOM OF GRANGE FELL ROAD before the land was built upon. This was the park and gardens of Hard Cragg, one time home of the Townleys who introduced the first Jersey cows into the area and, it is said, Beatrix Potter to the original 'Pigling Bland'. Photograph by H.T. Mason of Grange.

THE GRANGE NATIONAL SCHOOL BOYS AND GIRLS photographed in the 1880s. The school was opened in 1864, with Miss M. Marsh as mistress, and enlarged in 1880 when Thomas Ashley was the master.

THE *MIKADO* AT GRANGE in 1903, photographed by G. Wilson of Grange in the new Victoria hall which had opened in 1901. Grange and District Choral Society committee was Misses Gwatkin and Pearson and Messrs Broadbent, Gedye and Smith. The secretary was Mr Hawkrigg and treasurer Mr Nelson. The conductor was Mr Leonard Barton.

INSIDE THE 'WRITING ROOM' of the Northern Counties Convalescent Home of the North East Friendly Societies in about 1905. The manager stands at the drug cupboard with the matron, while an assistant leans on the scales at the back of the room. The residents pose in suitable ways. Note the manager's picture over the fireplace.

VIEWS OF THE GRANGE FELL OR CARTMEL ROAD about 1908 show the unmade road and the infilling development as Grange expanded; the first 'modern' semis had appeared. These scenes are much changed as development has continued and, of course, motor transport has had to be catered for.

THE BELL RINGERS from the Ulverston St Mary's parish church had many 'trips out' — they frequently rang the bells of other churches in the process. This outing, about 1930, was to Grange-over-Sands with a climb to the Hampsfell Hospice included. The chief bell ringer, Joseph Kitchin, is on top in a trilby. The hospice was erected in 1834 by a vicar of Cartmel, Thomas Remington, in appreciation of the delights he had enjoyed on the Fell. It would be difficult for anyone to express similar thoughts in this manner today.

THE VICARAGE AT LINDALE in Cartmel about 1910 when Revd T.H. Irving MA was curate in charge. There was (and is) confusion hereabouts as Grange-over-Sands, Lindale and Witherslack churches are all dedicated to Saint Paul so the records show 'Lindale parsonage' and not 'St Paul's vicarage'.

THE OLD MILL DAM AT LINDALE. W. and J. Mossop (see p. 23) of Grange-over-Sands had the mill at Lindale where they ground their own flour with power from a waterwheel. For many years their dam and weir were features of the village mentioned in guide books.

HOLLY HOUSE, Lindale about 1912, on a postcard specially produced by Keighley's Stores who occupied this building at that time. The postcard here is of interest as the photographer's title of 'Si-Ko' is that used by J. Simcoe and Son of Kendal.

THE LANE TO THE WINSTER VALLEY and Cartmel Fell at Lindale, photographed by Croslands of Arnside in about 1910. The business in picture postcards took many photographers into adjoining areas. The increase of the halfpenny postage rate to one penny after the First World War had a dramatic effect as postcards sales slumped.

'SUNSET' AT LINDALE in Cartmel, c. 1905, by Edward Sankey of Barrow-in-Furness. One of the many ways that local photographers made a living was by photographing houses. The owners then used the postcards to communicate with friends and family.

A VIEW OF LINDALE from the Grange road, photographed at the turn of the century by Crosland of Lancaster. In the background is the Commercial Inn (now the Lindale Inn) and on the right the memorial to John Wilkinson, the Ironmaster of Castle Head, who died in 1808.

THE FOOT OF LINDALE HILL. This hill was to become notorious for accidents when the main motor road to Ulverston and Barrow from the south came this way. Whitwell Marks and Co.'s Commercial Inn is having a beer delivery. Photographed by J. Simcoe of Kendal, probably for the Brewery, about 1910.

ELLERHOW was built by the Kendal architect Francis Webster in 1818 and was extended by his son George to make 'the perfect picturesque'. The Websters, masons and architects, originated at Quarry Flats, Cartmel, moved to Kendal in 1788 and re-established themselves in Cartmel at Black Rock and Ellerhow. Photographed by Wilson of Grange about 1905.

ABBOT HALL, KENTS BANK, a house which the Websters were concerned with as architects. In the first picture, by Brittain and Wright of Stockton, the donkey can be seen assisting with the lawn mowing about 1918 and in the second the donkey is seen at rest with a friend. One can hardly be as friendly with a motor mower.

THE ABBOT HALL was much altered over the centuries after the Reformation. It reputedly stood on the site of a grange of the monks of Furness Abbey, erected at a crossing of the sands. In 1915 it was purchased by the Methodist Wesley Guild as a guest house and has remained as such ever since.

KENTS BANK HOUSE, across the road from the Abbot Hall at Kents Bank, photographed by Edward Sankey in about 1914. Earlier this had been a ladies' boarding school. An inside view of the drawing room, taken at about the same time by A. and L. Slingsby of Grange, suggests the piano was the centre of the entertainment for guests.

on Lawn, Kents Bank.

GUESTS ENJOY TEA on the lawn at Kents Bank House about 1918.

MOORHURST HOLIDAY HOME sold postcards to guests and here we can see 'the road to Moorhurst' looking downhill to Kents Bank station, and the Guild Holiday Home dining-room – both about 1910. From 1822 this house had also been a 'high-class private boarding school'.

THE ENTRANCE GATES to Kents Bank House and the village post office photographed by A. and L. Slingsby of Grange about 1920.

KENTSFORD ROAD by Edward Sankey, about 1905, is 'the road to Moorhurst' from the other direction.

WRAYSHOLME TOWER, pictured by H.T. Mason of Grange before the First World War. The tower is said to have been built by the Harrington family in the fifteenth century but for many hundreds of years has been only a farm. In Victorian times the legend of the last wolf was rewritten as a love story, 'How the gallant Knight of Wraysholme rescued Beauty from the Beast'.

THE HOLYWELL OF ST AGNES on Humphrey Head has now lost its house, which was photographed by Edward Sankey about 1920. As Christians lost their interest in holy wells this site became a place of pilgrimage by the seekers of cures for bodily ills following many claims for the 'curative properties' of the water. In 1700 Dr Leigh records the well's reputation for curing 'jaundice, ague, worms and other diseases'.

THE OPEN DOOR OF THE WELL HOUSE, photographed by Atkinsons of Ulverston around 1902, with a variety of mugs and a jug for visitors to take the water. The key to the Well House was available 'at neighbouring Wyke farm'. There is no doubt that the waters would have some effect, although perhaps not that intended, as the spout bringing the water through the wall was made of lead. Castle Head and Humphrey Head together have many legends associated with them, as well as traces of ancient occupation. Humphrey Head is said to be the place at which the last wolf was killed and there is also an undoubted connection with early Christians. The area is certainly worth more academic attention.

ALLITHWAITE'S QUARRY, bowling greens and shop, another of Edward Sankey's photographs of about 1905. Housing has much altered this scene. The quarry was closed in 1939.

THE VILLAGE OF ALLITHWAITE from the fields with the church on top of the hill. The church dates from 1865 and was built with money left by Miss Lambert of Boarbank who also endowed the 'Allithwaite dole' for the poor of the parish. A guide book described Allithwaite as a 'cluster of villas delightfully situated on the shore of Morecambe Bay'. Photograph by Robinsons of Allithwaite.

WEST VIEW AND ASH MOUNT, Allithwaite, by Edward Sankey, in about 1910 when children could play in the road with no danger. The road and footpath were of dust and gravel.

ABIGAIL NELSON poses with her brother's motor cycle at Church View, Allithwaite in the 1930s. Abigail's grandmother can be seen later in the book as she was a Pepper from Home Ground, Coniston and the 'Langdale Linen industry'. Abigail's brother, Robin, was a partner in a firm of Grange estate agents.

THE NEW HOUSING ESTATE at Flookburgh West was started to house the workers at a nearby airship factory during the First World War. The scheme was never completed and the houses were taken over by Vickers of Barrow. The road names were taken from great battles of the First World War. Sankeys produced a set of picture postcards of all of the roads with their grim names. Here are Jutland Avenue and Somme Avenue in the 1920s.

THE ANCIENT TOWN of Flookburgh was also photographed by Edward Sankey. Here are two of his pictures. This was a Royal Borough of 1278 – the most important place in the whole area – but it never recovered from a fire in 1680 and has remained only a village.

TWO OF THE INNS in Flookburgh at the turn of the century pictured by Frith and Co. of Reigate. In the first the market cross faces the Hope and Anchor, when Emily Harvey held the licence, and the second shows the Kings Arms when George Fell was licensee. The Fells had the Kings Arms for some decades from the 1880s.

CARK RAILWAY STATION was the place where royalty and others visiting the Duke of Devonshire at Holker would alight from their train. Here the station is photographed by Friths about 1900, when passengers crossed the lines on a level crossing, before the footbridge was installed in 1908.

STATION ROAD, CARK, with The Engine Inn and hotel 'bus about 1912. Thomas Eyre was the landlord of The Engine Inn at the time. Photograph by Edward Sankey.

CARK HOUSE AND THE BRIDGE in another turn of the century picture of Cark by Friths. Cark House was the home of the Stockdale family who were involved in industry in the area and owned a mill in Cark. James Stockdale was an antiquarian who wrote *Annals of Cartmel*.

THE STAFF at the Cark railway station pose for the photographer in the late nineteenth century. The Furness Railway offered a secure career for many in the nineteenth and early twentieth centuries. Cark station is now an unmanned halt.

HOLKER HALL. The firm of Websters of Kendal had moved from Quarry Flats, Holker into Kendal in 1788 but returned to carry out major alterations to Holker Hall in 1840. On 10 March 1871 there was a fire which destroyed the 'new wing' which can be seen in the first picture, by Hogg of Kendal, about 1870. The second picture, after the fire in 1871, demonstrates how large sections of the wall were destroyed when the wood lintels over the windows burned through. It is reported that Lord Frederick Cavendish was awakened early in the morning by the mantlepiece in his bedroom falling. The fire engine from the Low Wood Gunpowder Works was brought in to assist the estate engine.

THE AUGUSTINIAN PRIORY OF CARTMEL was founded about 1188 and its church survived the destructions of the Protestant Reformation because it was the parish church as well as the Priory church. As it was, the choir was left open to the sky for eighty years. Cartmel Priory and Furness Abbey came into the hands of the Prestons of Holker who, in the mid-sixteenth century, would have happily restored them both to their previous owners but circumstances prevented that happening. The photograph is by Atkinsons of Ulverston about 1902.

THE INTERIOR OF THE CHURCH. Although the fabric of old churches is somewhat timeless, it is amazing the changes that do take place as these photographs show. In the first the choir stalls with their oil lamps can be seen in a photograph for W.H. Smiths, c. 1905, and the second, by Friths of Reigate, shows the nave with the huge stove that must have proved a penance to the churchwardens.

Carmel Church. Nave East.

THE CARTMEL PRIORY GATEHOUSE, c. 1900, showing the market cross used as a lamp post and the gatehouse used as an advertising stand for the Cavendish Arms. The shop of Robert Field can also be seen. He advertised as grocer and ironmonger. An early guide complained of the market cross being used as a bill posting station.

TWO PICTURES by Atkinsons of Ulverston about 1900 show Headless Cross from the Allithwaite road and the house which at that time offered 'apartments', 'tea and coffee' and 'teas and accommodation for cyclists' on various external notices.

THE COMMITTEE of the Cartmel races in 1920. Back row, left to right: Mr Grandy, -?-, Redmayne Rigg, Mr Heaton, Mr Orm and Major Young. Front row: Billy Dickinson, Mr Newby, Mr Wilson, -?-. Photograph by Hargreaves of Barrow-in-Furness.

THE SHAFTESBURY HOUSE, CARTMEL stall at the Stoneydale, Field Broughton Garden fête about 1912. 'Our Nation', 'God Bless our King and Queen' and 'Rest in the Lord' mottoes for sale.

CAVENDISH STREET, CARTMEL, by Friths of Reigate, shows the premises of William Ayers, which advertises itself as an 'old fashioned Eating House' and 'Family grocer and general caterers'.

LOOKING TOWARDS THE GATEHOUSE in Cavendish Street about 1900, by Atkinsons of Ulverston. The Cavendish Arms posting department is on the left, and Ayers' eating house on the right.

'THE BECK' AT CARTMEL was a very popular Friths postcard for many years, as was the picture of the Square, looking towards the Kings Arms hotel. Both views were on sale well into the 1930s when the views depicted had been changed greatly by motor traffic.

A POPULAR IDEA from Victorian times until the 1930s was to use a photograph of your house as a Christmas card. Here the 'Best wishes for a happy Christmas' comes with 'love from all at Cornbrook, Cartmel'.

AYNSOME AT CARTMEL by Atkinsons of Ulverston about 1900. The farmer is at work in front of the home of the Revd T.M. Remington. A small seed testing laboratory set up here by the Remingtons grew into an internationally famous analytical laboratory.

THE VICARAGE, CARTMEL, from the top of the Priory tower. This is another Atkinson's view from the turn of the century.

INSIDE THE GATEHOUSE. Lilywhite of Bradford, working for the LMS Railway, took this interesting view in the 1920s of the old schoolroom/court room in the gatehouse which, by that time, had become a museum.

ST PETER'S CHURCH at Field Broughton, Cartmel about 1900. In 1882 this church was described as having a nave and north transept and a small bell turret. Paley and Austin of Lancaster changed all that in 1892–4 when they erected this church with the obvious intent of its having anything but a small bell tower.

THE SOCIETY WEDDING on 20 June 1906 at Field Broughton church was that of Catherine Blanche Knowles of Broughton Lodge, seen here in her bridal coach at the front of Broughton Lodge, photographed by Mrs Sutcliffe of Burton-in-Kendal, who was herself listed as a guest at the wedding.

MISS KNOWLES was the daughter of Mr and Mrs J. Knowles of Kilnhurst, Todmordon and Broughton Lodge and the bridegroom was the Revd John Arthur Nash of Christ Church, Tunstall, Staffordshire. The Revd A.N. Crane of Perry Bar was best man. The happy bride and groom are photographed on the path in St Peter's churchyard by Mrs Sutcliffe.

CHARCOAL BURNING was a woodland trade carried out throughout High Furness and Cartmel. The same team to be found on p. 67 are seen here with their charcoal stack half made in the woods near Cartmel about 1905.

THE MAIN ROAD through Newton-in-Cartmel about 1905 with the school, which was also used as a chapel, on the left and the Crown Inn on the corner in the distance.

THOMAS BARROW'S SHOP at Newton-in-Cartmel, photographed by Atkinson of Ulverston, advertises 'licensed to sell tobacco, tea, snuff and coffee'. Thomas was also a farmer, joiner and wheelwright. Note the external curtain to keep the sun out.

NEWTON before the First World War, photographed by Sankey. The first photograph shows the cross roads at the Crown Inn and the second the sign post in the centre of the village. Note the peat and wood delivery from a cart.

SEATLE FARM, Newton in the late 1920s, by A.J. Evans of Preston, in another of the types of postcard/photograph intended for the family at the farm as well as a limited general sale.

THE FRIENDS MEETING HOUSE at Height, Newton-in-Cartmel was built in 1677 by Laurence Newton. George Fox records that fifteen years before the foundation, 'the rude multitude hauled me out, struck and punched me and threw me headlong over a stone wall'. Photograph by G. Wilson of Grange, c. 1905.

'APARTMENTS TO LET' is the title of this turn of the century photograph of woodcutters in the woods of Cartmel Fell. Bobbin, broom, basket and charcoal were all woodland industries that were extensively carried out in the Cartmel and High Furness woods (see also p. 80).

STAVELEY-IN-CARTMEL contains part of Newby Bridge (the rest is in Furness) and includes part of the shores of Lake Windermere where, at Fell Foot (see p. 76), Major Ridehalgh had a fine mansion. Here Sankey is satisfied with the view over the hamlet towards the Finsthwaite tower.

CHILDREN POSE in the playground of Cartmel Fell school. In the background is the Winster valley and, beyond, the Witherslack area of Westmorland. The school was originally erected in about 1720 and rebuilt in 1870. It was closed in 1965, when the building became the parish hall. Photograph, c. 1900, by C.I.C. Ltd (Renshaw series).

A GREAT WAR MEMORIAL STONE was dedicated in the churchyard of St Anthony's, Cartmel Fell in April 1924. Members of the Kings Own Regiment took part and are seen here presenting arms as part of the ceremony. The area had lost eleven men in the conflict. Two more names were to be added in 1945.

TWO VIEWS OF THE INTERIOR of the church of St Anthony (patron saint of basket makers and charcoal burners) at Cartmel Fell. The first dates from about 1900 and looks towards the plain altar. The second is of the 1904 harvest festival decorations. In 1987 thieves helped themselves to stools, a chair, a chest and a flagon that were treasures in this church.

J. TAYLOR OF THORPENSTYE HALL, another of the Taylor family, sent this christmas card to George Airey of Burblethwaite Mill in 1906 – 'A joyous christmas' was the message.

ANOTHER SEASONAL GREETING. Taylors at Tarn Green, Cartmel Fell also had photographs of their farm as Christmas cards in 1904. They wished all of the Clarkes at The Grove, Witherslack a Merry Christmas and a Happy New Year.

BURBLETHWAITE MILL, C. 1905. This remote mill was the home of the Airey family who were millers at the turn of the century.

THE MASONS' ARMS on Strawberry Bank was a resting place on the old road from Kendal to Ulverston via Bowland Bridge (which is nearby, but in Westmorland) and Gummers How. Situated half-way between Ludderburn and Cartmel Fell it was the 'local' to a large stretch of beautiful country with few inhabitants. John James Matthews held the licence when this photograph by Atkinson and Pollitt of Kendal was taken in the 1920s.

LOOKING DOWN from the unmade road over Gummers How in the 1920s on another Atkinson and Pollitt photograph. The village of Bowland Bridge and much of the background was in Westmorland. (See *South Westmorland Villages in Old Photographs*.) The River Winster was the Lancashire/Westmorland border hereabouts.

BIRKET HOUSES, Winster in the 1920s, photographed by J. Simcoe of Kendal. This was the home of the Birket family who gave Winster as their address when their house was in fact in Lancashire in Cartmel Fell parish.

LUDDERBURN lies behind Great Tower plantation, which the Boy Scout movement have made their own. It was to Low Ludderburn that the children's author Arthur Ransome came in 1925 and it was here he wrote *Swallows and Amazons* in 1929/30. This photograph was taken by Atkinson and Pollitt in the 1920s.

BROADLEYS. This house stands at the very top of Cartmel Fell parish, on the outskirts of the village of Bowness-on-Windermere. It was built for Leeds colliery owner Arther Currer Briggs by the famous architect Charles Voysey in 1898–1900 and, together with Moor Crag nearby, is now said to be the architect's best work. Here is a private photograph of part of the garden at Broadleys used as a postcard in 1910. 'Dear Carol, Do you like pinks — I wanted to jump in the lake yesterday it is so hot and sunny but I think it is a good thing I left my bathing dress in Wales.'

THE MANSION OF FELL FOOT was near Staveley-in-Cartmel and was for many years the home of Lt.-Col. George John Miller Ridehalgh. Its window overlooked the foot of Windermere lake and the steamer pier at Lakeside on the Furness side of the lake. The house was purchased in 1907 by Mrs Hedley who, intending to build on the site, pulled the old house down. The plans for a new house never came to fruition. The site is now a caravan park.

BIGLAND HALL, in a turn of the century view published by Woods of Haverthwaite around 1905. This had been the home of the Bigland family for many centuries.

AN INTERIOR VIEW of Bigland Hall with its clutter of antiques and curios, c. 1910. Photograph by Edward Sankey of Barrow.

THIS POSTCARD OF BIRK DAULT, near the Low Wood Gunpowder Works opposite Haverthwaite (the river was the boundary with Furness), was used as a birthday card in 1905. Birk Dault was built by Daye Barker, the founder of the gunpowder works, in 1798–9.

THE WORKERS' COTTAGES of the Low Wood Gunpowder Works in about 1914. The works were established in 1799 using water power for its mills and exporting powder to many parts of the world. Low Wood survived the takeover closures of local gunpowder mills when ICI became the owner in 1926 but was closed in 1935.

BOYS WILL BE BOYS on this turn of the century postcard, which also shows two of the many weirs which took water off to the various industries on the river.

CHILDREN FROM A NEARBY SCHOOL, possibly Greenodd, enjoying 'the seaside' at Mereness rocks on Mereness point in Upper Holker in about 1912. The Ordnance Survey, as is their way, wish to spell this 'Mearness'. We use the correct spelling.

THE WOODCUTTERS of the Cartmel Fells. As one of a series on Furness and Cartmel Rural Industries, Atkinsons of Ulverston published this picture showing a family hut with a low circular stone wall, and a turf-covered roof rising to a point on the wood poles supporting it. Coppicing the woods of Cartmel and High Furness and moving on when the woods had been cleared was a way of life that has disappeared in this century.

SECTION TWO

Among the Furness Fells

L.195. THREE SHIRE STONE, WRYNOSE PASS.

Lowe, Patterdale
Copyright

THE 'LANCASHIRE' THREE SHIRE STONE does not mention Cumberland and Westmorland. The stone was made a prominent landmark in the Lake District Association's proposal for a Wrynose–Hardknott new road in 1912. This was to provide the only substantial direct link from Wastwater and Eskdale to the eastern lakes, following the line of a Roman road.

COCKLEY BECK HOUSE AND BRIDGE, DUDDONDALE.
E.L.D.

COCKLEY BECK is a tributary of the River Duddon. Without it Wordsworth may have been less eloquent in his Duddon sonnets. The bridge in fact crosses over the Duddon. Photograph of about 1902 by Brittain and Wright of Stockton.

SEATHWAITE TARN nestles between Troutal Fell in the north-west and Dow Crag in the south-west. In 1907 the dam was built to enlarge the tarn and provide water for Barrow-in-Furness.

'WITHIN A SHORT DISTANCE OCCURRED THE NAVVY RIOT on July 25th 1904', read the caption on this postcard. Many other postcards were sold reporting the damage caused.

SEATHWAITE CHURCH was built in Victorian Gothic style in 1875 at a cost of £850 and replaced the old chapel where the renowned 'wonderful' Robert Walker was preacher for sixty-six years.

DALE HEAD lies on the road between Cockley Beck bridge and Birks Bridge at the foot of Grey Friar. This postcard was produced for J. Robson of Broughton-in-Furness post office.

'UNDERCRAGG', well named, was the birthplace of 'Wonderful Walker' in 1709. He and his wife were known as 'models of industry and thrift'. He ran a school in Seathwaite chapel and invested in the Newland Company near Ulverston. When he died, aged ninety-two, he left £2,000.

THE POST OFFICE and the grocers shop in Ulpha was held by the Tysons when this picture was taken at the turn of the century. Through its position on the river, Ulpha is strictly in the old county of Cumberland but merits inclusion as the hamlet has always been inseparable from Seathwaite and Broughton.

TWO DUDDON SCENES such as those that surely inspired Wordsworth. Many such postcards graced the albums of Edwardian romantics. A Duddon legend tells of a lady who was chased by a wolf and drowned in Lady's Dub at Ulpha. Now these scenes are a 'gully basher's' paradise.

Yarnbeck Pitchen,
Seathwaite.

DUDDON BRIDGE once linked Lancashire with Cumberland. It was formerly a packhorse bridge and before that the route was across the Duddon sands. Photograph by Sankey about 1905.

BROUGHTON MILLS is a hamlet 4 kilometres from Broughton-in-Furness and takes its name from a corn mill which utilized the River Lickle and where simple wooden agricultural implements were made. This is another postcard produced for J. Robson of Broughton-in-Furness post office.

THE FURNESS RAILWAY CONISTON BRANCH LINE from Foxfield also included a station at Woodland. The picture by Illingworths of Millom, c. 1912, shows two platforms, a passing loop of line and a signal-box with signal and staff. The post office was also in the station building. The trains of the period took 30 minutes to Coniston and 20 minutes to Broughton.

WOODLAND HALL. In the Mannex Directory of Furness and Cartmel of 1882, Woodland Hall was described as 'a pleasantly situated mansion surrounded by beautiful scenery', occupied by John Dodson de Skelton Esq., LLB, Camb and JP Cumberland. He was 'the largest landowner of the soil' in the area. This picture by Illingworth of Millom dates from about 1910.

BROUGHTON-IN-FURNESS RAILWAY STATION with the motorized rail unit, which worked the Coniston branch for many years, at the platform. Always in the front of railway innovation, the Furness Railway realized the value of the Railmotor units on their branch lines. The unit on the Coniston branch usually pulled one, and sometimes two, trailer coaches.

THE SQUARE at Broughton-in-Furness was constructed about 1760. This J. Robson postcard shows the obelisk erected in 1810 to commemorate the 50th year of George III's reign, and the four trees planted to celebrate Queen Victoria's jubilee. Also of interest is the Creightons motor bus on the local bus service.

TWO SCENES FROM BROUGHTON on postcards by G.F. Stengal and Co. show local pride in the Institute around 1909 and changes in level on the ground floor of the Old Kings Head and its neighbour. (No doubt all the ale flowed down to the gable end!) They appear to have managed a level first floor – perhaps the customers here preferred the horizontal.

THE SENIOR CHILDREN of Broughton-in-Furness School photographed by Albert Parker of the Sunbeam Studio, Blackpool in 1880. Each child was able to purchase the photographs in 'cabinet' or 'carte-de-visite' size. Taking 'Scholastic' photographs was good business for many early photographers. Broughton School, rebuilt in 1866, had George Henry Parkinson as the master when the photographs were taken. A number of the children are from the Coward, Newby and Whinneray families of Foxfield. Jonathan J. Coward, second from the right on the second row of the boys' photograph, was to die at fifteen years with 'the fever'.

FOUR UPRIGHT HANDBELL RINGERS of Broughton posing with clappers at rest in early Edwardian times.

FOXFIELD STATION on the Furness Railway, built in 1858, was the junction with the main west coast line and the Coniston branch. The first station was very small but this was enlarged in 1879 following plans by the Lancaster architects Paley and Austin. This early 1930s view is by Lilywhite of Sowerby Bridge.

THE COACH ran three times a day in 1889, taking a route from Ambleside to Coniston via the Yewdale valley. It passed Yewdale farm with its spinning gallery, perhaps now the most photographed building in the area. Redhead's of Coniston published this view of charabanc coaches after a visit to the waterfalls at Tilberthwaite.

HAND WEAVING.
LANGDALE LINEN INDUSTRY, CONISTON.
APPROVED BY PROF. RUSKIN.

ATKINSON'S SERIES.

THE 'LANGDALE LINEN INDUSTRY' at St Martins in Langdale and in the Tilberthwaite area of Coniston was started by John Ruskin in the late nineteenth century as a method whereby the local people could improve their lot by using their skills to produce lace and woven fabrics for sale. The Pepper family was at the heart of the industry and here Mrs Pepper (née Heskett) can be seen, as photographed by Atkinsons of Ulverston, at the loom at Home Ground Farm, Coniston about 1902.

CONISTON at the head of Coniston lake supports a long history. Its name is a hybrid of Old Norse for King's and Old English for town. Its prosperity due to copper mining, slate quarrying and later tourism produced a railway, part of which is seen here about 1920. The line, opened in 1859, was closed in 1962.

SOME OF THE SENIOR GIRLS at Coniston School in the 1880s when William Brocklebank was headmaster and Agnes Walker was mistress for the infants. The old school building was converted into the Mechanics Institute in 1854 when the new school was built.

NOTE THE SWAGGER and possessive pride of the motorists here who dominate The Crown Hotel at Coniston in the 1930s when Captain P.W. Powell was the proprietor. In 1938 The Crown offered room and board for 6s. 6d. single and full board 77s. 6d. per week.

WORKING TIMBER in the quarry at the top of the hill on the road to Coniston in the 1920s, photographed by Atkinson and Pollitt of Kendal. In the distance is the 'Alt Mein' or 'Old Man' of Coniston which was to become 'Kachenjunga' to Arthur Ransome's readers of *Swallows and Amazons*. This is the centre of the Arthur Ransome Country where friendships with local families produced the models for the characters in his childrens' stories.

JAMES PEPPER of Home Ground, Coniston in the 1880s when he was the clerk at Coniston railway station for the Furness Railway. James rose to be the general manager of a railway company in Northern Ireland. His family were at the heart of the 'Langdale Linen Industry' (see p. 94). Photograph by Shirtliffe John Priest, photographer of Barrow-in-Furness.

THE *GONDOLA* AND THE *LADY OF THE LAKE* photographed together at Waterhead pier, Coniston, c. 1910, by Raphael Tuck for the Furness Railway. The *Gondola* was in service from 1859 to 1939 and the *Lady of the Lake* from 1908 to 1939. The National Trust now have a replica of the *Gondola* on the lake.

SUNNY BANK, TORVER, pictured in 1910 by Sankey. Richard Charnley advertised 'Pick & Hammer Shaft Manufacturers, Spokes, Besoms etc.' Mrs Charnley advertised 'Apartments, Refreshments and Boats for hire'.

FLAG STREET, HAWKSHEAD (after 't' flags o'er t' beck' – slabs over the stream – had been replaced). Some of the most delightful picture postcards ever published of the Lake District were by the Hart Publishing Co. Ltd of London. Taken just before the First World War, the photographs usually included children and were very well reproduced onto postcards.

HAWKSHEAD HILL POST OFFICE, c. 1905, by Brunskill of Windermere: 'At Thomas Banks' letters arrive via Ambleside 9.00 a.m. and are despatched 6.45 p.m.'

THE CART and the delivery of coal by the roadside in Main Street, Hawkshead show customs very different to those of today. The dog is standing by the door of W. Hawkrigg's confectioner's shop – a family business dating back into the mid-nineteenth century.

HAWKSHEAD MANOR COURT-HOUSE, photographed about 1925 from the back although the normal 'tourist' picture would be from the front. The court-house is said to date back to the days of Furness Abbey but Mannex's 1882 directory reports that the building 'was rebuilt about 15 years ago'.

RIGGS OF WINDERMERE ran many coach services throughout southern Lakeland, and here their Windermere to Coniston coach is pictured at Hawkshead about 1905. This well advertised service was very popular with visitors as it included a crossing of Windermere on the ferry.

WRAY CASTLE (built 1840–7) was the 'holiday home' of the Potter family when Beatrix Potter was growing up. The castle dominates the Sawrey shore of Windermere but even William Wordsworth thought it 'dignified'.

HIGH WRAY POST OFFICE in the 1920s. Note the unmade road and the early Road Traffic Act 'school' sign. Postage on postcards had gone up to one penny resulting in a massive slump in postcard sales.

FAR SAWREY POST OFFICE as caught by Atkinsons of Ulverston about 1905. A letter up to 4 oz cost one penny postage; a 10 lb weight parcel ten pence; postcards $\frac{1}{2}$ penny.

THE INTERIOR OF ST PETER'S CHURCH, Sawrey in the 1920s, as pictured by Atkinson and Pollitt of Kendal. The church was built in 1869 on a site given by Joseph Garnett of Howe End.

HAYTIME AT NEAR SAWREY photographed by Atkinsons of Ulverston about 1905. For many years 'Miss H.B. Potter' – later Mrs H.B. Heelis – lived hereabouts.

TWO VIEWS of the Ferry Inn in the late nineteenth century before the Ferry Hotel was built in 1880 and the ferry boat service improved. Payne Jennings photographed one of the early paddle steamers at the pier when the signal to stop was a flag, and R. and W. Brunskill photographed the inn with the row boat ferry which was to be replaced by a steam ferry in 1870.

THE SEMAPHORE SIGNAL, which signalled to steamers travelling in both directions, is seen on the end of the Ferry Hotel pier at the turn of the century when the Windermere Yacht Races were based at the hotel. The postcard dated 27 June 1904 carries the comments, 'Doesn't it look like the seaside rather'. What would the writer think today?

THE POSTMAN calls at Satterthwaite in the 1920s. For many years at the turn of the century the Satterthwaite post office was 'at Mary Wilson's'. Letters arrived at 10.45 a.m. via Haverthwaite and were despatched at 3.10 p.m.; not the long working day of many post offices in the district.

FINSTHWAITE from Backarrow Road in the early 1930s, photographed by Raphael Tuck. Even then the road was virtually unmade.

HIGH FORCE FORGE at the turn of the century. At that time two bobbin mills – North and South – were working but the name of the area comes from the sixteenth-century forges on the site.

MAIN ROAD, Blawith in about 1910, by the Pictorial Stationery Company in their 'Peacock' series of postcards.

HAYMAKING AT LOWICK GREEN in the old manner with rake and fork. Backbreaking work and an overloaded cart.

THE CONISTON/SPARK BRIDGE/GREENODD ROAD JUNCTION in the early 1930s, showing the Farmers Arms Inn with the bus stop at the door. A very convenient arrangement remembered with pleasure by the authors. Photograph by Lilywhite of Sowerby Bridge.

NIBTHWAITE QUAY. Sankey of Barrow photographed many larger quay sides than that at Nibthwaite. Once at the heart of the rural industries of High Furness, and very much part of the Arthur Ransome country legends, this field at the southern end of Coniston was once busy with the copper and slate traffic to Greenodd port.

THE VILLAGE HALL at Spark Bridge in the 1920s by Lilywhite of Halifax.

THE 'OLD FACTORY' at Spark Bridge, with the Cotton Mill and Dickey Crag in the background. Benson and Cheetham's mill closed in 1867 but the building was used for other purposes until it fell into ruin after the First World War. It is reported that the building served as a drill hall for the Volunteers during the war years. Photograph by Middleton.

JACKSONS OF SATTERTHWAITE was one of many carrier businesses which provided an inter-community service in the days before the motor car and motor lorry. James Jackson advertised himself as 'Carrier to Ulverston, Hawkshead and Ambleside' in the 1880s and his son carried on the business.

THE INSTITUTE LODGE, C. 1919, in a postcard produced for J. Baythrop of the Institute Refreshment Rooms, Lakeside. Note the interesting open-top tourer motor car in the photograph by Lilywhite.

AT THE LAKESIDE PIER about 1919, also by Lilywhite for J. Baythrop. Note the railway lines for loading the steamers with coal from the coal store. The locally made swill baskets were used to convey coal on a small wagon from store to boat. In the background a small crane is being used to work timber from a barge.

THE STATION AND PIER AT LAKESIDE in about 1910, as photographed by Valentines of Dundee. The *Swan* (1869–1938) is under power at the pier while the *Tern*, built 1891, pulls away. The photograph was taken from either the *Cygnet* or the *Teal*. The railway station and pier were erected in 1869 by the Furness Railway.

THE CAFE AT LAKESIDE, when tea on the railway station veranda was very much part of the journey from Ulverston to Bowness or Ambleside. The building was demolished in 1970.

THE STEAM YACHT *BRITANNIA*, photographed by Raphael Tuck for the Furness Railway Company. Built in 1879, the *Britannia* was in Furness Railway ownership from 1907 to 1915 as a 'private hire' boat. She was scrapped in 1919.

NEWBY BRIDGE is a village divided by the river. The hotel and railway are in Furness, the smithy and post office in Cartmel. This view from 'the coffee room', c. 1910, when motor traffic was lighter than today, is from the Cartmel side of the bridge.

THE POST OFFICE at Newby Bridge was situated next to the smithy and run for many years by Thomas Wren, joiner, at the turn of the century. It must have been odd asking for a stamp in a joiner's shop. The message on the back of this card, sent to Miss Nellie Wrighton in Surrey for $\frac{1}{2}$ pence, reads, '25.8.1905. I am writing this at the Post Office.'

THE SMITHY AT NEWBY BRIDGE, along with the post office, was in the parish of Staveley-in-Cartmel as the River Leven was the boundary with Furness. The Bowerbanks were for many years the smiths at this busy smithy by the ancient bridging point where the river runs out of Windermere lake. Photograph by Atkinsons of Ulverston.

NEWBY BRIDGE RAILWAY STATION with a Furness Railway tank engine at the platform. Closed as a station in 1939, the Newby Bridge Halt saw its last through passenger train in 1965 before the branch was closed by British Rail. Ironically the station is now reopened on the private railway from Haverthwaite to Lakeside. Photograph by Sankey.

THE SWAN HOTEL, Newby Bridge, with visitors awaiting their carriages. A busy prosperous scene from about 1905. This hotel has Newby Bridge as an address but is in fact in Colton, a parish of Furness.

BOUTH HOUSE at Bouth, c. 1905, by Sankey. Also in the parish of Colton, this village has an old Norse (Norwegian) name meaning 'Herdsman's Hut' and was said to be originally the dairy farm belonging to Colton.

Anglers Arms, Haverthwaite

THE ANGLERS ARMS at Haverthwaite, c. 1905, when the main road to Ulverston from the south ran by the front door. Experimentations with 'Tar Spray' to hold the dust down on the unmade roads were then taking place and can be seen in this Valentine photograph.

HAVERTHWAITE STATION on the Plumpton junction to Lakeside branch of the Furness Railway, with an 0–6–0 tank engine as used by the Furness Railway on their branches. The proximity of the Backbarrow iron works and the Low Wood Gunpowder Works gave Haverthwaite a large goods yard.

ST ANNE'S CHURCH, Haverthwaite, c. 1905, by Atkinsons of Ulverston. The church was built in 1828 and had a vicarage adjoining until the A590 road improvements caused its demolition in 1971.

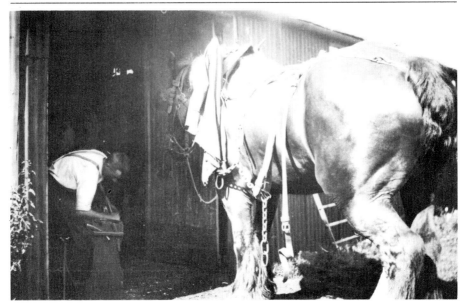

THE SMITHY at Greenodd, July 1936. An era was ending as more and more smiths became garage proprietors to survive, or closed down when horses ceased to be used for transport and work.

MAIN STREET, Greenodd in about 1902, outside Taylor's plumbers shop. This was the main road to Ulverston from the south until the new route on the site of the railway was built in the 1970s. Photograph by John Walker of London.

Ulverston, Dalton, Kirkby and Askam

WOODGATE HALL, Broughton Beck is in the parish of Osmotherly on the outskirts of Ulverston. The writer of the card, posted from Blawith post office in June 1902, confesses to having had lunch 'at this place'.

Ulverston, Newlands

THE NEWLAND VALLEY is steeped in industrial history, being the site of the first iron furnace in the Ulverston area in about 1747. This card, by Friths, of about 1918, erroneously uses the title Newlands for the Newland valley.

THE APPROACH to Ulverston's second railway station, c. 1910. The first station is reported to have blown down in a storm in 1855. This very fine station survives today with its clock tower being joined by a night club. Photograph by Valentine's of Dundee.

ULVERSTON STATION 'DOWN' PLATFORM with a board indicating that this was the junction for Lakeside and Conishead Priory. The Conishead Branch train ran from 1883 to 1916. The railway was originally planned to Barrow via Bardsea but was never completed.

FURNESS RAILWAY SHARP STEWART TANK ENGINE No. 78 (built 1873) draws into the platform at Ulverston station with a Barrow-bound train. This engine was scrapped in 1915.

The Last Train
Ulverston to Barrow

THE LAST TRAIN every evening from the south to Barrow was known as 'the whip'. This train's timekeeping and overcrowding were the subject of much gossip but depended on connections and time of year. This postcard by Cynicus of Tayport, printers of humorous cards, dates from about 1905.

ULVERSTON CANAL with a small coaster at the canal foot quay. This canal was opened in 1793 and served the town for many years. Its success was limited by the building of the port of Barrow-in-Furness in the mid-nineteenth century and the shifting of the Bay Channel.

AN AERIAL VIEW OF ULVERSTON, by Valentine's, shows the goods yard of the railway in the foreground when it was in extensive use. Much of the land in the background has been built on in the last few decades. The photograph can be dated to 1922 as the Palladium cinema is being built.

THE GARDEN DOOR of the County Hotel, photographed by J. Hargreaves of Ulverston, following the fire of October 1911. Mr Croston, a guest at the hotel, noticed the smell of burning in the early hours of 9 October and several residents had great difficulty escaping the blaze.

BROGDEN STREET, Ulverston, when the County Hotel and the first market hall were to be seen. The County Hotel was destroyed by fire in 1911 and the market hall was burned down in 1935. This view is now a cross roads on the new traffic route through the town.

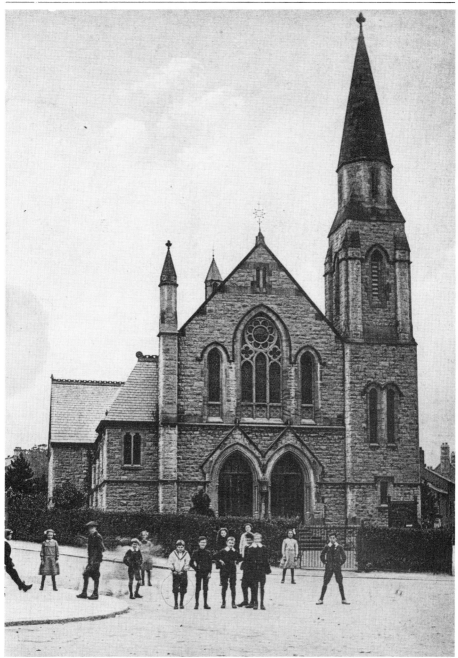

CHILDREN GATHER to watch the photographer on this Walter Benton of Glasgow photograph of the Ulverston Wesleyan Methodist church at the junction of Hartley, Neville and Chapel Streets, Ulverston. The church was opened in 1901 and the picture is dated c. 1910.

THE ULVERSTON COTTAGE HOSPITAL, c. 1903, by James Atkinson. This hospital was built in Newton Street in 1872–3, had its own committee of management, and was supported by the Hospital Saturday Parade.

A SCENE IN DALTONGATE, Ulverston at the turn of the century by James Atkinson shows Paradise Yard which is now a car park as all the mock-Gothic buildings have been demolished.

A STROLL ON THE ROPE WALK, Ulverston, alongside the Dragley Beck, by Mr Tom Bamber and his wife Annie (née Storey) and their dog. Tom was a 'drapers traveller' and lived at No. 13 Lightburn Road which, remarkably, is the same house where one of the authors spent his youth.

A VERY EARLY PHOTOGRAPH of the Hart Street Technical School, Ulverston. The school was built in 1900 on land owned by the old Town Bank Grammar school. Initially it was owned by ten Governors but the Lancashire County Council took over after the passing of the 1902 Education Act. The school site in earlier days was a tarn which gave the names Tarn Field and Spout Lane to adjoining land.

THE MARKET PLACE, Ulverston, when a very fine gas lamp graced the top of Market Street. In the background is the shop of H.W. Mackereth, seedsmen and publishers of the *Mackereth Year Book* from 1894 to 1902; this became the *Furness Year Book* with W. Holmes, of the Otto Printing Works, as joint publisher until 1909. This photograph from the turn of the century is by Stengal.

KING STREET, ULVERSTON, taken by Valentine's in about 1918. Note the lady on the left looking into the window of A. De Lucchi's Ice Cream Parlour and, on the right, John Smith's sign taking visitors into Smiths Court to his premises.

A TANK which was displayed in a special compound opposite Neville Street police station in Tank Square – now a traffic roundabout. It was after the First World War that Ulverston, in common with many other towns, acquired its vehicle (No. 2011). Here it can be seen on its arrival in 1920 with a crowd of people joining in the event. The tank remained a feature until the Second World War scrap collections.

THE ULVERSTON HOSPITAL PARADE at the Trustee Savings Bank corner in 1907. Florrie Werry and friend Janey ride horseback leading a mixed bunch of horsewomen and a Scots band.

PART OF THE CROWD awaiting the entertainment on the Hart Street Technical School field at the 10 May 1913 Hospital Parade. The Hospital Saturday Parade was introduced in 1899 to be held on Whit Saturdays.

HOSPITAL PARADE ENTERTAINMENT on the school field about 1910. Note the Hart Street post office in the background. Photograph by E. Roberts of Ulverston.

DECORATED CYCLES – much loved in Edwardian days – climb out of King Street into the Market Place on 10 June 1905. The event raised £348 2s. 8d., after expenses were deducted, and provided funds for additional bedrooms and enlarging the kitchen at the hospital.

SWARTHMOOR HALL, C. 1920, photographed by Dickinson of Ulverston. This building was where the Quaker movement was founded but it has been much altered over the years since the Fells owned it in the seventeenth century.

THE BOWLING GREEN at the High Carley Sanatorium near Swarthmoor when the fresh air treatment was considered the best for consumptives. In the background can be seen the huts and open ended wards used in this treatment. The hospital continued in use as a general hospital until the opening of the Furness General Hospital in 1984.

TWO VIEWS OF CONISHEAD PRIORY. The first by Atkinson shows the Hall in about 1902 when the building was a 'Hydropathic Establishment – recommended by high medical authority for summer and winter residence', offering lawn tennis, croquet, bowling and the 'Scotch game of golf'.

THE DINING ROOM at Conishead Priory after the building, in 1933, had become the Convalescent Home for the Durham Miners' Association. The stiffness of the regime can be seen; note the 'Silence' notice.

TIMBER WORKERS at Trinkeld (or Trinkelt — both names were used) when the sawing was by manpower and a double-handled saw. The name originates in the old Norse and means the spring of Thronder. The photographer was G.H. Horn of 10 Brook Street, Ulverston.

THE TARN AT URSWICK with a family rowing boat about 1905. This tarn has suffered badly with sediment from the Lindal area mines but has survived until our day in spite of predictions that it would be silted up.

PAGET'S PRIZE POSTCARD of Bankfield, Urswick in about 1910 shows what was for many years the home of the Wright family.

URSWICK CHURCH, C. 1905, showing the interior before the alterations which stripped off the plasterwork, and when the lighting was by oil lamp.

MAIN STREET, Great Urswick in the 1930s when it was much safer to herd a flock of sheep in the road that it is today. Photograph by Raphael Tuck.

A LADY CYCLIST pauses in Little Urswick about 1910. Note the unmade road.

BROW END, URSWICK is the title of this photograph by Sankey of part of the General Burgoyne Inn and the confectioners shop and refreshment room run by the Jenkinson family. The photograph dates from about 1910.

MILL HOUSE, BARDSEA, C. 1905. A very different scene to today. The postcard says 'There is no room inside as there is about eight people in a small room and one can't stir and two terrible kids. Bardsea is alright when its fine but in rain it is a terror'.

Sir Thomas Storey's Old School
Bardsea

SIR THOMAS STOREY'S OLD SCHOOL at Bardsea early this century. As the village 'was remote from any public school' Wilson Braddyll of Conishead endowed a school in 1781 but the inhabitants had to build it. Rent of a field called Long Croft provided the £8 each year for the master. In 1898 Sir Thomas Storey of Lancaster left £500 to be shared between the poor and the school.

THE SHORE ROAD at Bardsea in the 1920s, pictured by Valentine's of Dundee, with a postman avoiding the bus after buying an ice cream from the horse-drawn cart. This view is from the same position as Mill House earlier but looking in the other direction.

BARDSEA HALL at the turn of the century when it was in the occupation of Henry R.H. Gale Esq., JP. This Hall dated back to medieval times and had been the home of the de Bardsey and Wilson families. On the 21 August 1918 Colonel Henry Richard Gale sold the house and estate to Robert Bertrand Jackson, solicitor of Ulverston for £8, 950. It then came into the possession of Mr Chapman of Grange-over-Sands who, after selling off the woodwork and fittings to an American, demolished the house. Houses now occupy the site.

THE INTERIOR OF BARDSEA CHURCH about 1900 by Walton Porter of Ulverston. Holy Trinity, Bardsea was erected in 1843–9 using the famous Kendal architect George Webster. Note the rather plain oil lamps.

A PICNIC ON THE BEACH. When the Ulverston 'Honeypot' families went on a picnic to Bardsea beach about 1910 they did it in style with a large tea urn, best hats and all the children. The families are, left to right: Menzies, Simpson, Garnett, Boon, Wilkinson, Redpath, Kitchin, MacAlerney, Shuttleworth and Mackintosh.

ALDINGHAM'S ANCIENT CHURCH, dedicated to St Cuthbert, pictured by Atkinson of Ulverston in about 1902. The land between the motte and bailey castle on the coast nearby and this church is said to have been eroded by the sea and the village of Aldingham with it. Modern academics argue against this story.

THE CHURCH AT DENDRON originated in 1642 and has undergone much rebuilding since. The school was in the church until 1833. This photograph of about 1905 was used as a birthday card from 'Maud and Dave, September 1908'.

GLEASTON CASTLE AND FARM in a photograph by Hoskin dating from the 1920s. It is said that the castle was built by the Lords of Aldingham in the fourteenth century. It would seem the place had been falling down since the end of the fifteenth century. This ruin must be the most neglected ancient monument in the district.

GLEASTON MILL in about 1910 when Thomas Huartson was the miller. This picture shows the stream and mill house.

THE COAST ROAD, designed for the new motor traffic, was the wonder of the district when it was built in the 1920s. This view, showing a car approaching Roosebeck from Newbiggin bay, emphasizes the road sweeping along the coast.

PENNINGTON CHURCH from the turn of the century. Norcliffe's photograph manages to completely omit the road which is between the two walls in the centre of the picture. The church was rebuilt in 1826 but there is no doubt that the foundation is an ancient one, probably as early as any in the district. The best reference to its long history is to be found in Alfred Fell of Ulverston's *A Furness manor; Pennington and its Church*, published in 1929.

THE STOCKS have long been a feature of Pennington and are photographed here in the 1920s. Restored in 1924 by the vicar Canon George Kenworthy, these are amazing survivors as the use of stocks was banned in 1837. One would hope the restoration was for antiquarian and not penal reasons.

LINDAL RAILWAY STATION, photographed by Hoskins of Dalton, probably after the Furness Railway had been taken over by the LMS Railway. The station never recovered from the loss of the Lindal iron ore mines business and was closed in the early 1950s.

LINDAL VILLAGE in about 1910 shows, on the left, the church built in 1884 by the Dukes of Devonshire and Buccleuch and Harrison Ainslie, the mines' owners, and the green which replaced the small tarn which gave the village its name. The vicar at the time was the Revd A.P. Hayes.

THE SUNDAY SCHOOL FLOWER FESTIVAL approaches the church at Ireleth in 1907. The steep hill that can be seen took away some of the pleasure in participating in the festival.

THE RAILWAY INN at the corner of Dale Street, Askam. The inn, owned by Thompsons, was originally Nos. 22 and 24 Ireleth Road, but the mock-Tudor façade hides the two cottages. Sankey photographed the view, possibly when Edward A. Constable held the licence, just before the First World War.

ASKAM RAILWAY STATION in the early part of this century. Some of the station staff can be seen on the platform. This is now a unmanned halt. In the background can be seen the busy goods depot.

ANOTHER VIEW OF IRELETH ROAD, ASKAM from the R.A. Series, published by M.B. Cook of Askam post office in the 1920s. While a motor car can be seen, there is ample evidence of horse-drawn traffic.

THE ASKAM IRON WORKS with its famous 325 ft high chimney dominates the background of the Lilywhite photograph of the 1920s taken from the Kirkby Road, Ireleth. The iron works were founded about 1866 and by 1882 had four blast furnaces, two of which were the largest in the country. The depression of the 1920s saw the works closure.

BECKSIDE MILL, Low Quarter, Kirkby-in-Furness in the 1920s, showing the overshot wheel with the leet diverted off, and an unmade road.

SANDSIDE is the ancient port for the Kirkby area and saw much traffic in slates before the Furness Railway took the trade. This picture shows a deserted street with the Co-operative Store in the background.

SOUTERGATE, Kirkby about 1910, with early motor cycle and unmade road.

THE BURLINGTON SCHOOLS, Kirkby-in-Furness, c. 1902. The trim buildings show their source in the local slate quarries. The school was built in 1877 by the then Duke of Devonshire mainly for the children of the quarryworkers. Photograph by Atkinsons of Ulverston.

GEORGE ROMNEY, the famous artist, lived in the cottage at High Cocken shown in this Sankey photograph of about 1910. The Furness Railway restored the building into a Romney Museum and widely advertised the place, but Sankey's revealing photography shows how the house was almost lost to the quarry.

THE MARKET PLACE, Dalton-in-Furness in about 1902, with a gathering of local children. In the background is the Dalton-in-Furness Co-operative Society grocery shop called the 'Castle Shop'.

THE DALTON PARADE of 1910. G.W. Mitchell's photograph shows the local fire brigade proudly aboard their horse-drawn 'steamer' fine engine. Bulmer's Directory of 1910 shows W. Richardson as the fire superintendent – he was also the town surveyor and cemetery superintendent, living at 10 Fair View. W. Comber was captain – he was a builder with premises in Station Road and lived at 106 Market Street.

MARKET STREET, Dalton, c. 1910. The ladies and children gather outside the confectioners shop of S. Jardine, next door to Frederick Mitchell's fruiterers shop, in another of Mitchell's photographs.

MARKET STREET, Dalton, photographed higher up the road by Lilywhite in 1932. The cinema had appeared opposite the offices of the Dalton *Guardian*, Mrs Rule's tea shop and the shop of Hartley's, draper and gents outfitters.

TWO FINE FAÇADES in Dalton. Atkinson's photographed the Salvation Army Barracks at the end of Cobden Street around 1902 – the poster advertises 'self denial week'. The Picture Palace is photographed in 1913 to show the building before an upper storey was added. It eventually became 'the Roxy' with, next door, A. Brizzolari's confectioners, where 'the sweet toothes are satisfied'. This became known as 'Brizzy's'.

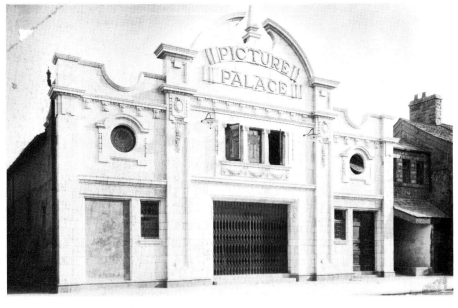

A SUMMER VIEW of the Roe Island pier for the ferry to Piel Island and its castle in the 1920s by J. Atherton of Barrow. This tip of Furness is an ancient port and the castle was the wool warehouse for Furness Abbey. Note the fine sailing boats used for ferrying across the channel.

ROE ISLAND RAILWAY STATION of the Furness Railway was at one time part of the port through which goods and people came into Furness. Barrow Docks, Heysham and Fleetwood took much of the trade in the nineteenth century but the railway, with the station at Roe island built in 1846, continued in use until 1936. The photograph was taken, as recorded on the postcard 'by Uncle Dick', 'from the watchhouse top', in the summer of 1905.

A ROUTE INTO FURNESS in Victorian and Edwardian times was via the Furness Railway steamers to Barrow from Fleetwood. Edward Sankey, the Barrow photographer, who was also the official photographer to the Furness Railway, found a lucrative trade in travelling on the steamers and taking photographs of the travellers from Barrow and from Fleetwood in the mornings and selling the prints on the evening sailings. He had processed and printed the pictures in his dark room during the afternoon. This group was photographed on the *Lady Evelyn* on 23 June 1914 on the morning return trip from Fleetwood to Barrow. Coaches and trains awaited at Barrow to carry the Blackpool holiday-makers to many destinations in south Lakeland.

THE PADDLE STEAMER *LADY EVELYN* of 1900 in a picture by Tucks for the Furness Railway. With the *Lady Moira* (built 1905), the *Lady Margaret* (built 1896) and the *Philomel* (built 1896), the Furness Railway ran a service to Fleetwood from Barrow until the time of the First World War when the *Lady Evelyn* and the *Lady Moira* became mine sweepers. After the war they were sold by the Furness Railway and renamed *Brighton Belle* and *Brighton Queen* to work the South Coast resorts. Both were lost at Dunkirk in 1940.

THE RUINED CLOISTERS at Furness Abbey, c. 1902, by John Walker of London. Since p. 157 the pictures have, in fact, been from within the Borough of Barrow-in-Furness, the subject of a forthcoming book in the series. We felt our book needed to illustrate this side of Edwardian Furness life.

ACKNOWLEDGEMENTS

The production of this book would not have been possible without the assistance, in various ways, of the following North Lancashire and South Cumbria folk:

Janet Dugdale of the Museum of Lakeland Life and Industry • Victoria Slowe, Director of the Lake District Art Gallery and Museum Trust
Christine Strickland and Sylvia Mallinson of the Kendal Library Local Studies Collection • Mrs A. Bonnett of Allithwaite • Mr W.R. Kendall of Pennington
Mrs A. Reed of Kendal, formerly of Allithwaite • Miss O. Wilson, formerly of Rigmaden

Our grateful thanks, too, to those people of the area into whose families this book intrudes, and to the many others who encourage and support us in the collection of local old photographic images.